AMERICAN PRESIDENTS

DONALD J TRUMP

INDIA JAMES

NorwoodHouse Press

Cataloging-in-Publication Data

Names: James, India.
Title: Donald J. Trump / India James.
Description: Buffalo, NY : Norwood House Press, 2027. | Series: American presidents | Includes glossary and index.
Identifiers: ISBN 9781978579750 (pbk.) | ISBN 9781978579767 (library bound) | ISBN 9781978579774 (ebook)
Subjects: LCSH: Trump, Donald, 1946---Juvenile literature. | Presidents--United States--Biography--Juvenile literature. | Businessmen--United States--Biography--Juvenile literature. | Celebrities--United States--Biography--Juvenile literature.
Classification: LCC E913. J36 2027 | DDC 973.933092--dc23

Published in 2027 by
Norwood House Press
2544 Clinton Street
Buffalo, NY 14224

Designer: Rhea Magaro
Editor: Kim Thompson

Photo credits: Cover, pp. 1, 7-11, 13, 15, 16 The White House; p. 4 V_E/Shutterstock.com; p. 5 Wikipedia; p. 6 f11photo/Shutterstock.com; p. 7 Library of Congress; p. 18 arikstw/Shutterstock.com; p. 21 Phil Mistry/Shutterstock.com;

Printed in the United States of America

CPSIA compliance information: Batch #CSNHP27: For further information contact Norwood House Press at 1-800-237-9932.

TABLE OF CONTENTS

Early Years

Donald John Trump was born on June 14, 1946, in New York City. He lived with his mother, father, and four brothers and sisters. For high school, he moved away from home to attend a private school in **rural** New York.

Building a Career

Donald graduated from the University of Pennsylvania. Then, he worked with his father in New York City.

The Trump family owned many buildings in the city. Some were apartment buildings and hotels. Donald and his father bought even more **real estate**. They built new buildings.

Donald became well-known. Newspapers and TV stations interviewed him. Their audiences were interested in what Donald had to say.

Donald liked being featured in the **media**. He starred in a TV show called *The Apprentice*. The show was about how to run successful businesses.

Donald decided to run for president of the United States. At first, he did not have much success. He tried to be elected in 2000, but he left the race before anyone could vote.

In 2005, Donald married Melania Knauss.

Donald ran for president again in 2016. His **slogan** was, "Make America Great Again." This time, he won the election.

Presidency

Donald was **inaugurated** as the 45th U.S. president on January 20, 2017. He began making changes to match his ideas. Donald thought that government should be run more like a business.

Donald put limits on how many people could come to the U.S. from other countries. He worked to remove people who were not in the country legally. He wanted to make more jobs for American workers.

COLD REDUCTION
APEX

G7
FRANCE
BIARRITZ
2019

Donald wanted the U.S. to be seen as a strong nation. He worked to make deals with other countries that would be good for America. He used what he had learned from business to help him govern the country.

Coronavirus
COVID-19
Vaccine
Injection Only
Coronavirus
COVID-19
Vaccine
Injection Only

In 2020, COVID-19 spread around the world. Donald directed scientists to develop a **vaccine** that would prevent people from getting the disease. They created a new vaccine in only 11 months. It saved many people's lives.

Second Term

In 2020, Donald ran for a second **term** as president, but he lost the election.

He ran again in 2024. During the **campaign**, a shooter tried to **assassinate** him. Donald won the election. He became the 47th U.S. president on January 20, 2025.

TEXT GEORGIA TO 88022
TRUMP
VANCE
MAKE AMERICA GREAT AGAIN!
2024

Glossary

assassinate (uh-SAS-uh-nate): to kill someone who is well-known or important

campaign (kam-PAYN): an organized plan to try and win an election

inaugurated (in-AW-gyuh-ray-tid): sworn in to begin work as an elected official in the government

media (MEE-dee-uh): forms of communication seen by many people, including TV, radio, and the internet

real estate (reel i-STATE): land and the buildings that are on it

rural (ROOR-uhl): of or having to do with the countryside; not urban

slogan (SLOH-guhn): a phrase or motto that expresses a belief or goal

term (turm): a definite or set period of time; American presidents are elected to a term that lasts four years

vaccine (vak-SEEN): a medical treatment that helps a person's body defend itself from infections

Thinking Questions

1. What city is most associated with Donald Trump?
2. What kind of business did Donald run with his father?
3. What TV show did Donald star in?
4. Why did Donald make deals with other countries?
5. How did Donald help prevent COVID-19 from spreading?

Index

About the Author

India James writes about science, technology, math, and history for young readers. She loves learning new things while writing books. India lives in Ohio with her family.